GIRL, GO GET YOUR LIFE!

A GOAL-GETTER JOURNAL FOR WOMEN WHO WANT MORE

Girl, Go Get Your Life!

A Goal-Getter Journal For Women Who Want More

Dr. Cherita Weatherspoon

Girl, Go Get Your Life!

Copyright © 2021 by Cherita Weatherspoon

ISBN 978-1-952870-02-6 (paperback)

All rights reserved. No part of this publication may be reproduced, distributed, stored in a retrieval system, or transmitted in any form or by any means, including photocopying, recording, or other electronic or mechanical methods, without the prior written permission of the publisher, except for brief quotations in critical reviews, articles, or certain noncommercial uses permitted by copyright law. For permission requests, write to the publisher, at:

info@cheritaweatherspoon.com

Quotes were found via Google® at: https://www.red.org/reditorial/10-inspiring-quotes-from-black-leaders-this-black-history-month; https://blackexcellence.com/black-women-quotes/; http://www.forharriet.com/2012/03/85-quotes-from-black-women-to-inspire.html; https://everydaypower.com/black-women-quotes/; https://cafemom.com/entertainment/210615-50-quotes-from-black-women

Legal Disclaimer

This book is for informational purposes only. The author makes no claims or guarantees of outcomes or success. The content in this book should not be considered as counseling or other professional advice. Readers may implement the information included at their own discretion.

Ordering Information

Books may be purchased in large quantities at a discount for educational, business, or sales promotional use. For information, email hello@spoonfedmotivation.com.

Work with Cherita

For information on booking Dr. Cherita Weatherspoon for speaking, enrolling in a coaching program, or to learn about Spoonfed Motivation Publications' author services, please visit www.CheritaWeatherspoon.com.

To my sisters, you deserve all that you desire;
so GO for it!

Rave Reviews

"Cherita Weatherspoon's GO formula provides us with an inspirational, practical, fail-proof guide for how to initiate the process of real change in our lives. Honest, deep, self-reflection is without question one of the disciplines that absolutely all successful people consistently employ in their lives and in their work. In quick, fun, immediately effective steps, this book gets you refocused, reflecting, motivated, and prepared to accomplish your goals and to change your life. You are smart to both read and share this book with your families, friends and the teams you lead because the strategies in it enable you to inject positive change into your business and into your life right away!"

-Je'neen Barlow
Author, Speaker, Executive Coach
Barlow Enterprises

"Dr. Weatherspoon offers ten practical steps to help the reader reach his/her goals. I found this book to be thought-provoking and inspirational. She challenges the reader to dig deep within to answer tough questions, thereby enabling the reader to push past obstacles. *Girl, Go Get Your Life!* is a simple, yet powerful guide to fulfilling your purpose. I can already see myself recommending this roadmap to friends and colleagues."

-Lisa Lewis
Vice President Seeds of Greatness Ministries
Founder *Girlfriends!*

"The GO strategy serves as a beautiful conduit for anyone who finds themselves stuck and stagnant between who they are now and who they ultimately want to become. As an entertainment correspondent, producer and content creator whose job is to deliver high profile in depth celebrity interviews across global multiple media platforms along with negotiating contracts with media elites in Hollywood, New York, and London, I have found the coaching offered in this book by Dr. Weatherspoon bar none. In order to execute at the highest level of my craft and sustain in the ever changing but always competitive space of entertainment news, it is imperative that I continue to implement the components of Dr. Weatherspoon's GO strategy. In a point by point layout that consists of awareness and accountability for one's own actions, Dr. Weatherspoon has successfully laid out a blueprint of characteristics that prepares the reader to want success, embrace success, and expect success. Her instructions require work and patience. But, more importantly, her instructions will guide you to the epicenter of opportunity and the ability to be like hinds and place your feet on high places."

-Tanisha LaVerne Grant
Independent Entertainment Correspondent

"From the start, I was drawn into critical reflection. Having spent years sifting through different tools for self-care, for help to live the life I want and am living on purpose and to be selfless in my care of the world around me, I found the very first step familiar, and necessary, and still drawn to think deeply about whether I have indeed grown as much as possible in regard to rising above past hurt and pain. Girl, Go Get Your Life! asks you to consider questions that may be unparalleled in any other coaching tool. 'Is whatever is holding you back WORTH giving away your power or sacrificing your dreams?' There are success superpowers and this book acknowledges that they are in you and helps you unleash them as if you are in life coaching sessions. This tool puts life coaching at the fingertips of millions and better yet, you can work through this process over and over and over again for any personal, professional or business goals. Get ready, get set, Girl, Go!"

-Rochelle Peterson-Ansari
Educational Leadership Specialist, Trainer Perceptions Unlimited

"Grab this book and guarantee the success you deserve. It is pining to generate wider and more succinct options needed to practically birth sustainable goals--yours! Dr. Weatherspoon has gifted the world with an unparalleled resource certain to weed out procrastination, underdog delay and bring balance to your success ladder. She masterfully devised thought provoking nuggets immediately followed by introspective "growth mindset" questions which jolt, challenge and catapult all willing to delve beyond today's sight lines. This GO 'force' will powerfully stand-up in you. The proof easily speaks through Dr. Weatherspoon's living witness, extends to her family success and thrives among all who adhere to Dr. Weatherspoon's counsel and coaching; gleaning in pursuit of purpose fulfilled! It's your time, now GO forth!"

-LaTerra D. Ruffin MDiv, CPE, CPMLC
Lead Pastor
Life Empowerment Church

"Girl, Go Get Your Life! is an amazing and powerful guide that will inspire you to press forward to accomplish your goals and live the life you desire despite the challenges that may be in your way. Dr. Weatherspoon has provided us with practical steps to take your life to the next level. If you're ready for the change you've been craving, this is a must read for you. Get ready to experience your breakthrough."

-Joyce Dungee Proctor
Speaker, Leading Career
Development Strategist, Coach, Author
Seminars By Joyce – The Total You, Inc.

Focus on what you desire, not on what you deserve. Your past failures and mistakes don't have to disqualify you from the future your soul is longing for.

— Dr. Cherita Weatherspoon

Contents

Acknowledgments ix
Foreword xi
Preface xv
Introduction 1
Goal-Getting Key 1: Get Over 7
Goal-Getting Key 2: Get On 15
Goal-Getting Key 3: Get Obsessed 25
Goal-Getting Key 4: Give Out 35
Goal-Getting Key 5: Grab Opportunities 45
Goal-Getting Key 6: Gather Others 53
Goal-Getting Key 7: Go On 63
Goal-Getting Key 8: Gamble Occasionally 73
Goal-Getting Key 9: Get Out of Your Own Way 83
Goal-Getting Key 10: Gaze Over 93
Goal-Getting Key 11: Goof Off 103
Goal-Getting Key 12: Grow Outward 111
Goal-Getting Key 13: Game On 121
MORE ABOUT THE AUTHOR 131

Acknowledgments

Thank you, God, for calling me to this work, and for not ending the call even when I refused to listen. To my husband, Gary, who allows me to dream and to do, I love you. To my children, Emile, Corban, Jaden, and Ian, thank you for giving me the time–your time–to do what I've been called to do. Thank you to the women who have motivated me simply by being who they are and stepping out in faith and on purpose; you never know who is watching or how much of an impact you are making. Thank you for forging the path.

Foreword

When you think about goals and the real steps to accomplishing them, I believe we can all share an experience of things we've tried in the past. After all, if you felt like you had a handle on achieving your goals, you probably would have never considered picking up this book; however, because you did, it tells me a couple of things. First, you have goals that you would like to accomplish and just haven't met them yet; and second, you have done it all before - had a goal, started on a path to achieve it, followed the goal plan, and then... crickets; another year has passed and you still have that same "dream deferred."

As a teacher of goal-setting and manifesting dreams, I thought I had explored every aspect of how to accomplish them. In *Girl, GO Get Your Life*, Dr. Weatherspoon has developed a phenomenal strategy for creating lasting change in your life by taking it to the next level. These 13 steps are not goal-setting as usual. It forces you to **Reflect**, which allows you to explore your thoughts and feelings, **Identify** what you have done or what you plan to do, **Clarify** by exploring a new perspective, and **Act** by creating a practical action plan to implement your newfound knowledge.

The writing exercises after each brief lesson allow one to explore the things you really need to consider. Science concludes that writing about your goals helps make sense of what you are working toward and what may have prevented success in the past. The physical act of writing down a goal makes it real and tangible. You have no excuse for forgetting about it. This book, though, is more than just SMART goals. The *Act* step is often missed in the process of goal-setting. You get so focused on the outcome that you forget to plan all of the steps that are needed along the way. By writing it out as you read, you will literally be crossing each one off as you complete it, you'll realize that you are making progress towards your ultimate goal. This is especially important if your goal is big and demanding. *Girl, GO Get Your Life* will set you up for long-term and life-changing success.

If you're tired of trying to achieve your goals in the same way you've been taught and coming up empty, then this book is for you. It is a new approach that, if followed, can significantly change your life.

Goal-setting is much more than simply saying you want something to happen. If you clearly define exactly what you want, understand why you want it in the first place, and with this book explore the deeper things that may be holding you back through journaling, the likelihood of your success is greatly increased.

Dr. Cherita Weatherspoon leads by example and *Girl, GO Get Your Life* comes from her very own recipe book of success. By following the steps detailed herein, you can set goals with confidence and enjoy the satisfaction that comes along with knowing you achieved what you set out to do.

Allison T. Butler
The Prison Break Coach

Preface

There is an art and a science to goal-getting. (Yes, you read that correctly, goal-getting NOT goal-setting. We can all set goals, but we don't all get the goals we set.) The science is in planning your goals and the art is in the execution of the steps needed to accomplish your goals.

The SMART acronym that is taught and used by millions of people to set their goals is an excellent tool. However, setting goals is just part of the process. The magic–the art–of goal-getting lies in what you do after setting your goals. That process looks different for everyone and it often requires more than just taking action. Many of us will have to deal with both internal and external "stuff" so we can take the action necessary and get over the hurdles that we will inevitably face as we journey towards our goals.

Girl, GO Get Your Life! was written to help you deal with that stuff; and it was written as a result of my learning how to deal with my own stuff.

Whether it was fear, perfectionism, a lack of support, confusion, overwhelm, or any of the other myriad challenges I faced (and sometimes still face) on my way to accomplishing my goals and manifesting the life I envision for myself, my family, and those I was called to impact; I had to learn to move forward, to go, in spite of it.

That's what I want to help empower you to do. To go! Because everything you imagine, everything you desire, everything that is already prepared for you is on the other side of your decision to go get it.

Introduction

It is one thing to talk about and envision your future and to know where you want to go, but it is a totally different thing to know how to get from where you are to where you want to be. It is one thing to develop SMART goals and know the steps to take to accomplish your goals, but a totally different thing is to know how to deal with the challenges that you will face as you work towards meeting your goals.

You see, no matter how well you can write out or state a SMART goal, it is not enough to move you from where you are to where you want to be. Having a plan is not enough. Having an accountability partner, a mentor or friend who can help keep you on track, is not enough.

I am not telling you not to set goals, not to make sure they are SMART goals, not to write them down, not to plan, or not to find people to help you along the way. What I am telling you, however, is that there are going to be challenges that come your way and threaten to thwart your progress, get you off track, and in some cases totally destroy you. Some of these challenges will come simply because of the goals you have set, some will come because of decisions and choices you make that are not in your own best interest, others will come because some of the people in your life will not want to see you "make it," and still others will come simply because challenges, issues, and problems are a part of life and everyone has something to deal with. No matter how good a person's life may seem from the outside looking in, I can guarantee you that everyone has had some stuff to deal with as they have worked towards reaching their goals.

So, if everyone has some stuff to deal with, why is it that some people accomplish what they set out to accomplish and others do not? Why are some people successful while others fail? I believe it is because some people understand what the GO, G - O, in goal really means.

Girl, GO Get Your Life! is designed to help you deal with the stuff that keeps you from setting or accomplishing your goals. Through this life application journal, you will identify the things (and people) that have been distracting and deterring you. You will learn to release emotional baggage, relax and enjoy YOU, and you will develop the skills and the fortitude to make it into that small percentage of people who actually set and get their goals.

But, remember, for real change to occur, you will have to take action. You will need to do something —you will need to *GO!* This life application journal will help you do just that. My recommendation is to read through each step before going back to complete the journal entries. This will give you a clear understanding of the process and allow you to see how the steps work collaboratively to move you forward. Keep in mind that while this is a process and there are steps involved, the steps do not necessarily occur in sequential order. You may not work totally through one step before beginning the next; and some steps, like Gaze Over and Goof Off, are steps that you should repeat throughout the process. Adapt these steps as a continuous and perpetual approach to achieving your goals.

In each step, a description of what is necessary to move forward is provided. You are then asked to **Reflect** on what you've read–sharing both your thoughts and your feelings. Then you'll move to very powerful and pointed questions that will help you to **Identify** the things that have been influencing you, holding you back, distracting you, or otherwise inhibiting your progress. The next section asks questions that will help you to **Clarify** where you are now and how you want or need to move forward. Finally, each step asks you to **Act**.

It is your commitment to taking the time to respond to these questions and then to implement them in your life that will make the difference in where you are today and where you will be 12 months from now. It is a small thing that brings about a major impact. It won't take a lot of time, but it will take a lot of heart. This is soul work. Are you ready? I'm with you, so girl, let's GO!

Dr. Cherita

Success is an intentional outcome of planned priorities and committed action.

— Dr. Cherita Weatherspoon

GOAL-GETTING KEY 1

Get Over

Sometimes you've got to let everything go–purge yourself. If you are unhappy with anything... Whatever is bringing you down, get rid of it. Because you'll find that when you're free, your true creativity, your true self comes out.

— Tina Turner

Are you living a fairy tale life? Do you have everything you could dream of and would not change one thing about your life? Or, have you been disappointed or hurt by people you love and care about? Do you feel like life has not been fair to you? If so, this first step is for you.

Get Over.

Whether it was a friend, lover, parent, sibling, spouse, boss, or co-worker–whoever it was that hurt you–Get Over it. Whatever you didn't like, whatever made you mad, or whatever the unfair situation; Get Over it. No, you did not deserve it. No, they did not apologize. Yes, you are angry and it still hurts; but hanging on to whatever it is, is only hurting you. Focusing on past, and even present, pain will keep you from your future goals. Whatever that thing is that has you constantly talking and thinking about yesterday, last month, last year, or five years ago… Get Over it.

Getting over it doesn't mean you forget about what happened, but it does mean that you rise above it. How do you do that? Let's get to work.

React

What is your immediate reaction to what you've just read? What thoughts came to mind? What feelings did you experience?

_____
_____
_____
_____
_____
_____

Identify

Who are the people that hurt you that you have not forgiven?

_____
_____
_____
_____
_____
_____

Why is it difficult for you to forgive them?

___

Have they moved on from the problem/situation? How do you know?

___

Clarify

What benefit does not forgiving them bring you?

What are you missing out on because a part of your life - a part of your heart - is stuck in the past?

Is it worth it? What is it about this person or this situation that makes you willing to give away your power and/or your joy?

Act

Speak your PEACE. If the person is accessible and it is safe for you to do so, talk to them directly. Otherwise, it is just as powerful to verbalize this while looking in a mirror or at a photo of the person. Say the following, filling in the blanks based on your experience:

I feel hurt when

_____

_____

_____

I felt

_____

_____

_____

and it has bothered me since it happened. But today, I am letting it go. I can no longer give your actions any power in my life. I can no longer allow this situation to continue to bring me pain. I forgive you, and I also forgive myself for not letting go of this anger and hurt sooner. I am worth so much more than this.

If this isn't enough for you, go to a private place, throw something, yell, cry, cuss; but whatever you do, make the decision (and it is a decision) to Get Over it. Clinging to the past and holding unforgiveness in your heart does not serve you in any positive way.

Don't talk about the person or the situation again. Don't let other people pull you into a conversation about it. When it creeps into your mind, speak aloud, "I am over it. It is not worth my time or energy." Then say this short affirmation:

I am free from anger and fear. I am guided by love and I forgive freely. Because love fills my heart, good things come my way.

I'm convinced that we Black women possess a special indestructible strength that allows us to not only get down, but to get up, to get through, and to get over.

— Janet Jackson

Goal-Getting Key 2

Get On

*Forget WHAT you became. Today,
become WHO you were created to be.*

— Dr. Cherita Weatherspoon

After you Get Over, it is now time to Get On. Get On with your life. Begin to live like you have a future beyond your current or past situation because you do. It is not enough to get over something–to rise above it; while you may be operating at a higher level, you are still lingering in the same general area. Maybe you have stopped talking about whatever it was. You may have even forgiven the wrong that was done to you; but you are not ready to try again, to trust again, to love again.

After you Get Over, you have to Get On with it. You have to be about making the life YOU want to live, not the life that just happens to be thrown at you. Get On with going back to college. Get On with getting that job at the company you have always wanted to work for. Get On with relocating to *that* city. Get On with starting *that* business you have been planning on paper for all these years. Get On with turning your side hustle into a legitimate business. Get On with introducing yourself to that person you see every day at lunch, church, or wherever, that always smiles at you, but you are too afraid to respond because of the person you just realized you needed to Get Over. Get On with it. Get On with living your life.

React

What is your immediate reaction to what you've just read? What thoughts came to mind? What feelings did you experience?

_____

_____

_____

_____

_____

Identify

Where do you feel stuck in life; like you just can't get past this point?

_____

_____

_____

_____

_____

_____

What do you think is holding you back?

What is it that you want to do that you have not pursued?

What prevents you from pursuing those things?

If you could wave a wand, how would your life be different?

Clarify

Look at your previous answers. Are the reasons you stated about being stuck and not pursuing what you want within your control or out of your control? How?

If you believe the reasons are out of your control, think deeply about it and identify one action you can take in each area (where you are stuck in life and what you want to pursue) that can impact the situation in a positive way.

_____

_____

_____

_____

_____

_____

How will your life be different if you take these actions?

_____

_____

_____

_____

_____

_____

What do you see in your future if you don't take these actions?

_____
_____
_____
_____
_____
_____

Why are you worth taking action?

_____
_____
_____
_____
_____
_____

Act

Write a deadline for completing each of the actions you listed under *Clarify* above. The deadline must be within seven days. If there is no possible way to complete the action within seven days (example: start college classes, but you are reading this in October) break the larger task into several smaller tasks and complete at least one of them in the next seven days, and continue working on completing these tasks in 7-day increments until the larger task is completed.

Area of Stuckness	Action	Deadline

Once completed, describe how it feels to have taken action in these areas.

_____

_____

_____

_____

_____

Keep moving forward. Continue to identify areas where you want to move forward in your life and Get On with it. It can be in your work, relationships, family life, business, or any area in which you feel unfulfilled. Write those things below. You don't need to take action on all of them right now; but write them down as a reminder and after you have accomplished one of your first goals, come back to this list to get started on the next area.

_____

_____

_____

_____

_____

_____

It's time for you to move, realizing that the thing you are seeking is also seeking you.

— Iyanla Vanzant

Goal-Getting Key 3

Get Obsessed

> *I have learned over the years that when one's mind is made up, this diminishes fear; knowing what must be done does away with fear.*
>
> — Rosa Parks

You have gotten over the past hurt that kept you from looking towards your future and you have made the decision to start living and pursuing the things that you desire, but you have to get serious about going after what you want. Make a commitment to this pursuit.

Get Obsessed.

Think about your goals. Spend time planning out the steps you need to take to get where you want to be. Spend time each day doing something that gets you closer to your goal. Treat your goal like it is your new lover, your favorite sport, show, or another pursuit you love and invest in. Spend your free time on *it*. Talk about *it* to others, think about *it*, talk to yourself about *it*, turn things down that keep you from spending valuable time on *it* and that do not contribute to your success with *it*. Get Obsessed with *it*. Make *it* the number one priority in your life (after God and your family). If you are not working on your goal, be learning more about what you need to achieve *it*. Research *it*, feed *it*, and nurture *it*. Get Obsessed with *it*. You will know you are obsessed with *it* when people around you complain that *it* is all you talk about or that you are spending all your time on *it*. If you are not hearing that, you are not obsessed. You might have a crush on *it*, but you are not obsessed with *it*.

React

What is your immediate reaction to what you've just read? What thoughts came to mind? What feelings did you experience?

_____

_____

_____

_____

_____

Identify

What is *it* for you? What is the big dream?

_____

_____

_____

_____

_____

_____

How much time are you currently spending on *it* on a daily basis? How about weekly?

_____
_____
_____
_____
_____
_____

Who knows about *it*? Who have you shared *it* with? (No, you cannot share your dreams with everybody, but you need to share *it* with somebody; otherwise *it* is a secret and there is no accountability for you.)

_____
_____
_____
_____
_____
_____

Clarify

Why does *it* matter to you?

_____
_____
_____
_____
_____

What are you willing to do to make *it* a reality?

_____
_____
_____
_____
_____

How will *it* change you or impact the world?

_____
_____
_____

Act

Find time to work on *it*. Schedule this time on your calendar like you do other appointments. Make *it* a priority. This should be reflected in your schedule. When will you work on it?

Find two people who you can trust with your dreams and ask them to be your accountability partners. One person should focus on holding you accountable for sticking to your schedule (share your schedule with them–just the days and times that you should be working on *it*) and the other person should be focused on your progression– what and how much you are accomplishing.

Who will hold you accountable for sticking to your schedule and how will they do that?

Who will hold you accountable for making progress on *it* and how will they do that?

Speak life. Say something positive about *it* every day. What is your affirmation?

_____
_____
_____
_____
_____

Bring life. Do something related to *it* every day. What are you committed to doing on a daily basis?

_____
_____
_____
_____
_____

Be passionate and move forward with gusto every single hour of every single day until you reach your goal.

— Ava Duvernay

Goal-Getting Key 4

Give Out

Service is the rent that you pay for room on this earth.

— Shirley Chisholm

The first three steps were rightfully and appropriately selfish, but this step is about other people. While the achievement of your goals is pretty much up to you and you have to put in the work, the reality is that no one does it on their own and it is not likely that others will help you if you are not willing to help others. Be willing to Give Out.

Give Out of your heart. Give Out of your talents. Give Out of your pain. There is someone who can use your help. It may be directly related to your goals, or it may simply be your presence for someone who is lonely, your words for someone who needs encouragement, your skills or talent for someone who cannot do something quite as well as you can. It may be volunteering with an organization or mentoring someone younger, or simply showing kindness or compassion. Giving Out can take on many forms and it can be something big or small. It can be something you do every day or something that is done on a certain occasion. But whatever it is, whatever you have to offer (and you do have something to offer), Give Out of yourself to others and you will find that others, perhaps not the same people you helped, but others will give out of themselves to you.

React

What is your immediate reaction to what you've just read? What thoughts came to mind? What feelings did you experience?

Identify

List your skills and talents.

How can you use your skills, talents, time or money to help someone else?

What groups of people do you want to help?

What causes are important to you?

What organizations can you connect with that will allow you to use your skills, talent, time and/or money to support the people or causes that matter most to you?

Clarify

How could sharing your skills, talent, time and/or money enrich someone or a cause that matters to you?

How can this experience benefit you? What do you gain by giving out to others in this way?

How will you know that you have made a difference?

Act

Write down three to five organizations, groups, individuals or entrepreneurs that you know could benefit from your skills, talents, time or money.

_____

_____

_____

_____

_____

_____

_____

Contact each of them and offer what you have to give (skills, talent, time or money). Do not ask how you can help or if they need help. Be specific about what you are offering (for example: developing their marketing materials for free, volunteering at their upcoming event, being a mentor with their youth program, presenting a workshop on choosing the right college, donating $100 to cover the cost of registration for a teenager to attend a leadership conference). The goal is to do something that matters to you in a way that utilizes your unique value while also benefiting the entity or person receiving from you.

In what way can you help each of the organizations, groups, individuals, or entrepreneurs you listed above?

___

___

___

___

___

Be diligent and do not give up. It may take some time to work through approval processes but keep calling until you have solidified the plan to Give Out or until you have been told no.

After you've completed your service, describe how being of service, giving out, felt to you.

___

___

___

___

___

___

Now, set another date to do it again, either with the same organization/person or a different one to whom you can be of service.

If you get, give. If you learn, teach.

— *Maya Angelou*

Goal-Getting Key 5

Grab Opportunities

*Don't sit down and wait for the opportunities to come.
Get up and make them.*

— Madam C.J. Walker

When you develop your goals, you should have a plan for accomplishing them. However, your plan should not be so rigid that you cannot see how people or experiences outside of your plan can help further your progress towards your goals. Your plan cannot be so inflexible that it does not permit you a little discomfort when faced with something that is unfamiliar. You have to be willing to Grab Opportunities.

When it makes you nervous and takes you out of your comfort zone, Grab Opportunities. When it takes you into unfamiliar territory, Grab Opportunities. They may come when you least expect them, in a different form than you thought, and from a place or person that you never would have expected.

But do not turn away from opportunities because they were not a part of your plan. Plans can change, plans do change, plans will change. Control that change as much as possible by being open to unexpected opportunities. Don't turn away opportunities because it is different or new. That is what makes opportunities what they are. Do not turn away from them, grab them.

Don't mistake opportunities for distractions or distractions for opportunities. Distractions typically show up in the form of something that interests you or something that you should do because it's the right thing to do, but they do not directly relate to your goals or help push you closer to your goals. Distractions take your time, energy, and effort away from the pursuit of your goals. Opportunities, on the other hand, directly relate to your goal, help to advance your progress, expand your network, or build your skills and knowledge as it relates to your goals. Avoid distractions, Grab Opportunities.

React

What is your immediate reaction to what you've just read? What thoughts came to mind? What feelings did you experience?

_____
_____
_____
_____
_____

Identify

What opportunities have you let pass you by because it did not fit in with your timeline or plan?

_____
_____
_____
_____
_____
_____

What opportunities have you missed because you did not think you were ready?

What opportunities did you turn away because you were afraid?

What opportunities are open to you now?

What are you doing now that is a distraction from your goals?

Clarify

Making the choice to not take advantage of opportunities is typically for one of two reasons: control or fear. Either you want to be in control of what happens, when it happens and how it happens or you are afraid that it will not work out. If you did not create or initiate the opportunity, "it's not the right time," or you "don't have the time." If you are afraid, you wonder: "Can I do it?" "Am I ready?" "What if?" Yes, these could be legitimate reasons and questions, but often they simply are not. They are excuses. So, what is your excuse? What prevents you from being open to new opportunities?

What is it about things not going as you planned that bothers you?

Why are you afraid?

Act

When an opportunity comes your way, ask yourself the following questions:

1. *Is this related to my goals?*
2. *Could this increase the knowledge or skills I need to accomplish my goals?*
3. *Could this help me meet people who will help push my vision forward?*
4. *Could this propel me forward in the journey towards my goals?*
5. *Have I been preparing for this opportunity?*

6. *Will anyone die if I do this?*
7. *Will I lose my job or damage a relationship with someone I love if I do this?*

If the answers to questions one through five are yes and the answers to six and seven are no, grab the opportunity.

Identify two to three recent opportunities that you did not take advantage of. Go back to the people who offered you the opportunities and ask if the opportunities are still available. List them on the next page and write down the outcome.

_____

_____

_____

_____

_____

_____

Dreams are lovely. But they are just dreams. Fleeting, ephemeral, pretty. But dreams do not come true just because you dream them. It's hard work that makes things happen. It's hard work that creates change.

— Shonda Rhimes

Goal-Getting Key 6

Gather Others

No matter what accomplishments you make, somebody helped you.

— Althea Gibson

Sis, you are absolutely brilliant! I have no doubt about that. And, you are likely the epitome of "superwoman" BUT no matter how great you are, you can't do it all by yourself. You can't get to the ultimate goal on your own. And, you shouldn't try to do it by yourself. Gather Others.

You bring a lot of value to the table, but no matter how good you are, you still need other people. Can you experience success doing it by yourself? Yes, you can. Your success, however, will be so much greater and you are likely to experience it much sooner when you have a team with you. You need team members in a variety of different roles. You need those who are working right beside you on your goals. These may be volunteer assistants, employees or independent contractors, partners, or other roles that are doing work to advance your goals. You need those who are rooting for you to accomplish your goals. These *may* be friends and family or biz besties. You need those who are supporting you in accomplishing your goals. These may be coaches, consultants, or mentors. You need pinch-hitters, those who can step in and bridge the gap when you can't meet the demand. These may be baby-sitters, chaperones or drivers, or housekeeping, laundry or meal services. You need those who are going to keep you accountable to your goals. This may be a coach, mentor, friend, or biz bestie. And, you need those who are going to pray for you and with you, encourage you, and lift you up, reminding you of who you are and whose you are.

So, girl, Gather Others in pursuit of your dreams. Yes, you may have to pay for some of your team members. But you are worth the investment. Your team members should not be chosen out of convenience but out of commitment and capability. There will be those who want to be on your team but can't because they either lack the commitment for the role or because they are not capable of meeting the requirements of the role.

There are resources waiting to come your way; if only you were open to accepting them in the way they show up. You can operate in excellence without being exclusive - excluding people who don't think like you, act like you, or want to be like you.

While your mission, your goals, and your impact are all about you, they're really not about you at all. Be open. Be accepting. Be inclusive. Give other people a chance. Forgive. Love. Recognize your own stuff. Be reflective. Be compassionate.

Don't be disappointed by those you thought were on your team who you find are not supportive of your goals. Rotate them out to a better position (or no position at all) and keep it moving. If you haven't found the support you need or the team you need, it's because you're not looking hard enough or you keep placing people in the wrong role because of your unspoken and perhaps inappropriate expectations. Voice your needs and be open to however and in whoever the resource shows up. Whatever you do, don't do it alone. Gather Others.

React

What is your immediate reaction to what you've just read? What thoughts came to mind? What feelings did you experience?

___

Identify

What team members do you already have in place that are performing well in their roles?

___

What team members are failing to meet your expectations? Should they be on your team and in that role?

_____
_____
_____
_____
_____
_____

What roles do you still need to fill to have the support you need to accomplish your goals?

_____
_____
_____
_____
_____
_____

Clarify

In what areas of your life do you need the most support right now? Is it family and relationships, career or business, health and wellness, social or cultural, financial, spiritual or ethical, or mindset, mental health or education?

_____
_____
_____
_____
_____
_____

What type of support do you need?

_____
_____
_____
_____
_____
_____

Where can you get the support you need?

_____
_____
_____
_____
_____
_____

Act

What is the first area of support you are going to address?

_____
_____
_____
_____
_____
_____

What is the first step you are going to take to address it?

_____
_____
_____

When are you going to complete that first step?

What is the outcome you are seeking?

How will you know when it is accomplished?

What can you do to maintain the outcome?

Surround yourself with only people who are going to lift you higher.

— Oprah Winfrey

Goal-Getting Key 7

Go On

Just be honest and true to yourself. If your friends around you love you, they'll wish you the best and want only what's going to make you happy.

— Meagan Good

As you make progress towards accomplishing your goals, you are going to find that some of the people whom you thought cared about you start to think differently about you. You might hear them say things like, "You're changing," "You think you're better than everybody," "Since she started (<u>fill in the blank</u>) she ain't got time for nobody." That one is my favorite; because the thing is, they are right. You ain't got time for nobody, but you do have time for anybody who is trying to be somebody.

You will change and that is a good thing. In fact, it is a great thing! These people do care about you, but they are not sure what your change, your progression, and your goals mean for them. They are afraid that you will leave them behind.

But you must know this one thing, you are not leaving anyone behind. They are choosing to stay behind. You, however, must Go On. Go On, despite what they think. Go On, despite what they say. Go On, because they cannot live for you. Go On, because you cannot live for them.

Everyone has a choice to make about their lives and you cannot be, nor are you responsible for, another person's choices. If they choose to advance with you, hold out your hand and walk side-by-side towards your goals. But, if they choose to stay behind, you must Go On without them.

React

What is your immediate reaction to what you've just read? What thoughts came to mind? What feelings did you experience?

Identify

Who or what causes you to hesitate about making changes in your life that will advance you to the next level?

What is so good about where you are now that you are willing to consider giving up everything waiting for you in your future?

_____

_____

_____

_____

_____

What will you miss out on if you decide to stay behind instead of going on?

_____

_____

_____

_____

_____

Clarify

How does playing small, staying who you are and continuing to do what you have been doing serve you?

_____

_____

_____

_____

_____

How does it serve those you love? (Hint: It does not, even if they think it does. You can be a much greater help to them if you become who you were created to be.)

_____

_____

_____

_____

_____

_____

If you stay behind, how will you feel about the people who discouraged you five years from now when you are stuck in the same situation that you are in today?

Act

Talk. Talk with the people you love who you feel are discouraging you from pursuing your goals. Find out why they are doing it? Share how it is affecting you. Reassure them that they can come with you, but that you must Go On. Share how it will impact you if you do not go after what you want. Then ask about their dreams and desires—what it is they want to do. Encourage them to take the first steps towards making their dreams a reality. Set a date to talk with them and write those dates below.

Describe how it felt to have these conversations.

___

Describe how you feel now about working towards your goals.

___

Guard your heart. If after talking with them, they continue to discourage you or they are generally unsupportive, limit what you share about what you are doing. Do not give them the opportunity to discourage you or to sabotage you. Only share your goals and progress with those who will nurture them and help protect them. What if it is your spouse or significant other? If this is the case, you want to encourage healthy communication. Try developing a reasonable agreement around whatever their concerns are and establish boundaries that are respectful to both of you. Write below what you were able to come up with.

_____

_____

_____

_____

_____

_____

I don't have any time to stay up all night worrying about what someone who doesn't love me has to say about me.

— Viola Davis

Goal-Getting Key 8

Gamble Occasionally

I don't like to gamble, but if there's one thing I'm willing to bet on, it's myself.

— Beyonce' Knowles Carter

When you are working towards a goal, you will have to make decisions along the way. Some of these decisions will be very clear cut and it will be easy to know what you should do. Other decisions will not be as clear or may involve some risk. Be willing to Gamble Occasionally. Now, I don't mean to risk everything you have for a "sure thing," but I do mean that you need to be willing to take some risks to advance your cause. You will not always know what the outcome of a decision or choice will be. You will be called on to risk time, to risk effort, to risk money, and every now and then you will need to take that risk and Gamble Occasionally.

"What if" is a wicked game. What if I do this? But, what if I do that? What if this happens? But, what if it does not?

None of us knows for sure what the future holds, but we do know that not taking any action means that you will not progress. Too many people choose not to act out of fear of loss or failure.

Risk is not a bad thing. You just need to be smart about the risks you take. Do your homework, ask questions, weigh probable scenarios, and then make an educated and informed decision. Don't take unnecessary or crazy risks, but be willing to Gamble Occasionally when the reward outweighs the risks. And, when you don't know what to bet on, bet on yourself.

React

What is your immediate reaction to what you've just read? What thoughts came to mind? What feelings did you experience?

Identify

Describe a risk related to your goals that you did not take.

Why didn't you take the risk (be specific)? Was it fear of failure, fear of embarrassment, fear of success, or something else?

___

If you had taken the risk and it was successful, how would your life be different?

___

If you had taken the risk and it failed, what is the worst thing that could have happened? What was the likelihood of that happening?

How could you have recovered from it?

Clarify

What have you lost or delayed because you were not willing to take a risk?

_____
_____
_____
_____
_____

Why do you believe that you, your dreams, your goals and your desires, are not worth taking a risk?

_____
_____
_____
_____
_____
_____

How valuable are your dreams, goals and desires to you if you are not willing to take risks to make them a reality?

_____

_____

_____

_____

_____

_____

Are you willing to risk living the rest of your life unfulfilled, dissatisfied, and full of regret?

<u>Yes</u>   <u>No</u>

Unfulfilled
Dissatisfied
Full of regret

Act

If your answer to the last question was no, then make a decision to take a small risk now. Put yourself first for once. Try taking a day off from work to put time and effort into your dreams. I promise you, the company will not fall apart in your absence.

How are you going to put yourself first?

_____

_____

_____

_____

_____

Reach out to someone who could mentor or coach you, or in some way provide some expertise that would help you progress. Who is this person and how can they help you?

_____

_____

_____

_____

_____

Market your product or services. Put it out there, if only to get feedback to help improve what you are doing. So, what are you going to put out there?

_____

_____

_____

_____

_____

_____

Face the fear and do something. What will it be?

_____

_____

_____

_____

_____

_____

I'd rather regret the risks that didn't work out than the chances I didn't take at all.

— Simone Biles

Goal-Getting Key 9

Get Out of Your Own Way

*There's always something to suggest that you'll never be
who you wanted to be.
Your choice is to take it or keep on moving.*

— Phylicia Rashad

If you're like most women, you probably have plenty of reasons to be hesitant about going after what you want. You've likely been conditioned to think a certain way. You've probably had at least one experience where your intelligence or capabilities have been questioned. You've likely been looked down upon, treated badly, been unappreciated, and undervalued somewhere along your journey.

These types of experiences can shape our perceptions of who we are and who we can be. But because your soul is yearning for more, you are becoming uncomfortable with the lies you've been taught to believe. Something in you is beginning to recognize the truth and the power of who you are.

But when things get challenging, you fall back; you regress. And YOU become your biggest hurdle to success. Girl, Get Out of Your Own Way!

I get it. Imposter Syndrome is real. I've experienced it in the past and it still creeps up every now and then. What I learned to do and what you must learn to do is recognize it and then attack it by finding the truths that invalidate the thoughts.

What do I mean by that? For whatever thought or belief that is keeping you from moving forward, identify experiences you've had, positive words that have been spoken to you, results you've produced, the knowledge you've gained, and skills you've developed, that are evidence that the thought or belief you have is false. For example, if you think that you're not good enough to be a motivational speaker, identify times when you've spoken in front of people and received good feedback. Think about when you've encouraged someone with your words and they've thanked you. Look for things that prove the negative things you believe or think about yourself to be wrong.

You can also find evidence in other people. For example, if you think that someone from your background can't do a certain thing, find someone who has a similar background that is doing what you want to do. If you think that no one will buy what you want to sell, find someone who is already selling something similar. If they can do it, so can you.

The lesson here is that everything you need for your next step is already inside of you. You just need to tap into it and use it. I firmly believe that God will not give anyone a vision He has not equipped them to start building and for which He will not make provision for its completion.

The problem is rarely outside of us. It's the internal struggle to be our authentic selves, to believe in the power of who we were created to be and to be able to stand boldly in that even when it directly conflicts with what the world or other people say or believe about us. And, so we become the trip hazard in our own lives; the thing that causes us to stumble repeatedly.

Decide today to believe that you are all that you know deep in your soul you are and then act on that belief. I promise you that you will absolutely love her and the life that she creates for you. Girl, Get Out of Your Own Way!

React

What is your immediate reaction to what you've just read? What thoughts came to mind? What feelings did you experience?

_____

_____

_____

_____

_____

Identify

List three beliefs you have about yourself that you know are holding you back.

_____

_____

_____

Where did those beliefs come from?

_____

_____

_____

What evidence do you have that these beliefs are false?

Clarify

What do you need to believe about yourself to accomplish all that you desire to accomplish?

Based on your response above, what is the truth? Write a positive and affirming statement that communicates the truth that you will stand on from this moment forward.

Now that you know the truth, what is possible for you?

Act

Start each day by reaffirming the truth of who you are. Speak out loud the statements you wrote above. Speak them in the present tense using "I am" statements.

_____
_____
_____
_____
_____
_____

Find a small group of women you can trust; with whom you can share your internal struggles, and who will remind you of who you are when you forget. These may not be women you are currently connected to. Be open to the possibilities within new relationships. Be able to give this same kind of support in return. Who are these women?

_____
_____
_____
_____
_____

Show up for yourself every day. What that looks like each day may vary, but do something for yourself or in support of your goals each day. List at least five things you can do to show up for yourself.

We must reject not only the stereotypes that others hold of us but also the stereotypes that we hold of ourselves.

— Shirley Chisholm

Goal-Getting Key 10

Gaze Over

The ability to take pride in your own work is one of the hallmarks of sanity.

— Nikki Giovanni

After Getting Over, Getting On, Getting Obsessed, Giving Out, Grabbing Opportunities, Gathering Others, Going On, Gambling Occasionally, and Getting Out of Your Own Way you have probably made quite a bit of progress towards your goals. This is the time to stop and Gaze Over where you have come from and how far you have come.

Look at how your attitude has changed, how much more confident you are, how strong you are, how much closer you are to your goals. Look at the people who have shown up in your life to help you after you made the decision to change your life. Look at the doors that have opened for you since you decided to *GO* for it.

Every now and then, along the path towards your goals, take time to Gaze Over everything that is now behind you and that which lies ahead of you. Take a survey of your life and note that when you decided to live the life that you desired and deserved, the ground rose to meet you, and the path before you opened up with each step you took forward in spite of what you saw in front of you. This will help to re-energize you and strengthen you for what lies ahead. Gaze Over.

React

What is your immediate reaction to what you've just read? What thoughts came to mind? What feelings did you experience?

_____

_____

_____

_____

_____

Identify

What are some of the decisions you have made recently that are moving you closer to accomplishing your goals?

_____

_____

_____

_____

_____

_____

What are some of the actions you have taken that have helped accelerate your progress?

_____
_____
_____
_____
_____
_____

Who are some of the people you have connected with that have motivated or encouraged you?

_____
_____
_____
_____
_____
_____

List three things that you have accomplished.

_____

_____

_____

_____

_____

Clarify

Think about the challenges that you have faced. How does it make you feel to have accomplished what you have in spite of those challenges?

_____

_____

_____

_____

_____

Now, think about how much closer you are to your goals. Describe how it feels to know that soon you will be living your dreams.

_____

_____

_____

_____

_____

_____

Write below why you deserve this... because you do deserve this.

_____

_____

_____

_____

_____

_____

If you don't feel like you have accomplished much, take the time to reassess. Consider how important this goal is to you. Think about how you have been spending your time. Have you really been putting forth the time, energy and effort necessary to accomplish your goals? Have you been caught up with distractions rather than opportunities? How can you get back on track? What things have you been doing (or not doing) that aren't working for you?

_____

_____

_____

_____

_____

_____

Act

Take a deep breath. Now, begin to visualize what it will be like to accomplish your goals. What are you doing? How do you feel? How has it changed your life?

_____

_____

_____

_____

_____

_____

Do this whenever you need to encourage yourself or whenever you are facing a challenge in accomplishing your goals.

Everything is worth it. The hard work, the times when you're tired, the times where you're a bit sad, in the end, it's all worth it because it really makes me happy. There's nothing better than loving what you do.

— Aaliyah

GOAL-GETTING KEY 11

Goof Off

Caring for myself is not self-indulgence. It is self-preservation, and that is an act of political warfare.

— Audra Lorde

Deciding to *GO* for your goals typically means hard work, persistence, and a loss of social and free time. So, every now and then you have to take time to Goof Off.

You do not have to wait until you have accomplished the goal. You need to reward yourself along the way and celebrate the small accomplishments that are getting you closer to the overall goal. After all, life is about living, not just accomplishing goals. Life should be fun. So make sure that you build some time to Goof Off into your plans. Otherwise, you risk Getting Overwhelmed (this is NOT one of the steps in the process; you should avoid this), having your health impacted by stress, feeling distanced from those closest to you, and maybe even feeling disappointed after you have reached your goal. Have fun, de-stress, take a break. This is self-care.

Learn to care for yourself as you care for others. Recognize that the more you care for yourself, the better equipped you are to accomplish your goals and to impact the world in the way you were created to do it. While this can include a beauty regimen, it is really much more than that. This is about rest and rejuvenation. It is about keeping yourself full so that when it is time to pour out, you have something to give.

Don't depend on others to help you find time for self-care or to recognize when you need it. If you act like a superwoman, people will expect you to be a superwoman. When you need help, ask for help. When you need a break, take a break; even if it means that you have to put the plans in place so you can take the break. Powerhouse woman, sometimes you have to turn the power off so you can reboot. Learn to live light and live to laugh.

React

What is your immediate reaction to what you've just read? What thoughts came to mind? What feelings did you experience?

_____

Identify

What do you like to do that you have not been able to do in a while?

_____

Who do you like to spend time with that you have not seen in a long time?

_____

_____

_____

_____

_____

How do you like to treat or pamper yourself?

_____

_____

_____

_____

_____

Clarify

Have you been working hard? How?

_____

_____

_____

Have you made progress? How?

Have you been consistent? How?

Have you been making self-care a priority? How

What is keeping you from letting loose and taking time to refresh?

Act

Take some time for yourself. Sleep in late, watch movies all day, go shopping, go out with friends. Whatever it is, do something that is fun. Then do something that is relaxing. What are you going to do and when are you going to do it? How often will you do it?

___

Plan to do something to reward yourself for the progress you've made along your journey. What are you going to do and what is the benchmark for doing it?

___

When I'm tired I rest. I say, "I can't be a superwoman today."

— Jada Pinkett Smith

Goal-Getting Key 12

Grow Outward

Instead of looking at the past, I put myself ahead twenty years and try to look at what I need to do now in order to get there then.

— Diana Ross

On this journey to your goals, you will come across many situations and challenges that will give you the opportunity to learn and grow. Whether you do will depend on your mindset and how you respond to those situations. Choose to Grow Outward.

Growing Outward means that you tap into the woman you need to be to overcome or triumph in that situation. This helps you to get through the current trial but also prepares you for the next trial. It shifts the focus from what is going on or who is doing something to you to what you can do to make the situation better, to bring resolution, or to prevent it from happening again.

Growing Outward also means that you recognize what is already in you but also who you need to become on the way to accomplishing your goals. You do indeed already have everything you need within you for your next step but you may not yet have it for your 20th step. If you can envision who you need to be farther down the path, you can make the most of the challenges and situations that come your way, recognizing that there is always a learning experience to be gained regardless of the outcome.

It's important to recognize that the outcome does not determine whether you grow or whether there is an opportunity for growth. The opportunity exists whether you are victorious in the situation or not.

Consider what worked for you, not just what worked against you. Think about what you did do, not just what you didn't do. Reflect on your responses and interactions and recognize what helped the situation and what hurt it. Don't focus on the "others" in the situation. You likely have little to no control over them. Focus on you because that is the one thing you can control and should always have control over. Own your stuff, all of it, whether it's good or bad. Then learn the lesson so you can grow from it and become better because of it.

There is truth in the saying, "Trials come to make us strong," but some trials keep coming because we never learned the lessons we were supposed to learn from them. If we don't learn the lessons and don't grow, it delays the accomplishment of our goals. Getting to your goals will require you to grow towards your goals.

React

What is your immediate reaction to what you've just read? What thoughts came to mind? What feelings did you experience?

_____
_____
_____
_____
_____

Identify

Reflect on a past experience and the lesson you learned. How did that lesson prepare you for where you are now?

_____
_____
_____
_____
_____

How do you think that lesson might be applied in different situations you may face in the future as you get closer to your goals?

Reflect on a different past experience that left you angry, hurt or resentful. What lesson could you have learned from that experience had you been less focused on how you felt about it?

Clarify

When you envision yourself accomplishing your goal, how do you see yourself? Who do you need to be at that moment?

_____

_____

_____

_____

_____

_____

What areas of growth do you need to focus on to become that woman?

_____

_____

_____

_____

_____

_____

Given those areas, what challenges can you anticipate facing that would help you grow in those areas?

Act

When you are facing a challenge, what steps can you take to shift your focus from the challenge to the lesson you can learn from the challenge?

How can you evaluate whether you've grown from an experience? What evidence would exist to prove that you are a different (better) person in this particular area of growth? Consider what other people might say, what the outcome of the situation might be, how you would respond, and other things that would demonstrate that there has been some growth on your part.

Celebrate your growth. When you have learned a lesson that resulted in significant growth that is helping you to get closer to your goal or in becoming the woman you desire to be, celebrate it. Personal growth is nothing to take for granted. So many people choose the easy route staying the same because growing tends to be uncomfortable. So, when you've faced yourself and decided to become a better version of yourself, you deserve to be celebrated. What are three things you can do to celebrate your growth?

_____

_____

_____

_____

_____

You will be wounded many times in your life. You'll make mistakes. Some people will call them failures but I have learned that failure is really God's way of saying, "Excuse me, you're moving in the wrong direction." It's just an experience, just an experience.

— Oprah Winfrey

GOAL-GETTING KEY 13

Game On

*You don't make progress by standing on the sidelines,
whimpering, and complaining.
You make progress by implementing ideas.*

— Shirley Chisholm

Key 13 brings us to a point of new beginnings. Game On. You've accomplished a goal, now I want you to determine the next goal that you are going to commit to working towards today. It does not matter how big or how small it may seem or how important or valuable someone else may think it is. It simply has to be something that YOU want to accomplish and you have been too afraid to try, have lacked confidence, other people have talked you out of it or said that you could not do it, or you just have not made time to focus on it. Identify what that next goal is and declare today, Game On!

You've proven that you can play the game, so be in it to win it. Continue to suit up and get on the field. You cannot win if you do not continue to play. If you play and do not win, you will learn some things that will make you better and stronger for the next game (goal). But you have got to be in the game to have a chance to win the game.

React

What is your immediate reaction to what you've just read? What thoughts came to mind? What feelings did you experience?

Identify

How have you been preparing for this time in your life?

In what ways have you practiced for your turn at success?

_____

_____

_____

_____

_____

Who are your cheerleaders (supporters, motivators, encouragers)?

_____

_____

_____

_____

_____

Who are your coaches (advisors and mentors)?

_____

_____

_____

Who are your fans (people who believe and find value in what you have to offer)?

Clarify

Why is it your time?

Why do you deserve to be successful?

What impact will achieving your goal have on the world?

Act

Get your game face on. Get focused, get serious, get in the game. Minimize your involvement in activities that do not, in some way, contribute to the knowledge and skills you need to accomplish your goals. What are you going to let go of or turn down to focus on what you need to do?

_____

_____

_____

_____

_____

_____

Show up for the game. If you are nervous, show up anyway. If you are afraid, show up ready to play. If you feel like you are not ready, show up and get ready. If other people play better than you, show up ready to learn all that you can. If you play better than everyone else, show up ready to coach. What does showing up look like for you?

_____

_____

_____

___

___

___

Play the game. Get in there and get it done. In spite of obstacles and challenges–play. If you have to be a one-person team–play. If you have to coach yourself and cheer for yourself–play. Playing the game is the only possible way to win the game. Winning is what you want, but losing is better than having forfeited (giving up without even trying). Keep playing, eventually, you'll end up a champion.

Are you ready to play? Game On!

You are on the eve of a complete victory. You can't go wrong. The world is behind you.

— Josephine Baker

MORE ABOUT THE AUTHOR

Dr. Cherita Weatherspoon is a Profit Strategist, Business Accelerator, Publisher, Speaker, and Author. Through her Powerhouse Coaching brand, she coaches women on launching and growing a six-figure expert business so they can make an impact while making a significant income.

Her mission is to engage, elevate and empower women in life, business, and career. She engages women through shared experiences, humor, and sometimes tears; challenging them to move, act, and overcome on their way to becoming.

Her desire is to elevate their way of thinking - to think about possibilities rather than probabilities; what can be rather than what has been; and who they can become rather than the identity they feel they've lost.

Ultimately, Cherita wants to empower women with practical strategies, a plan of action, accountability, and support to accomplish their goals and live the life they desire - without the overwhelm and overworking.

Cherita holds a bachelor's degree in Business Management, a master's degree in Student Affairs in Higher Education, a doctorate degree in Educational Leadership, and an Educational Specialist certification. She is also a Certified Professional Coach and a Certified Job & Career Transition Coach. Having been published numerous times, she is an International Best Selling Author.

As a wife and mother of four who also worked full time and served in her community, Cherita understands the demands on educated and highly skilled women and how those demands keep us from going after the things we really want in life. In 2016, after a successful 20+ year career in higher education administration, Cherita faced a life-changing decision: take another executive leadership position or take a chance on herself. SHE CHOSE HER.

Now Cherita is living out her calling to impact change in the lives of women as a coach, publisher, author, and speaker.

Her journey continues, and while it hasn't been easy, it's been worth it. She's worth it!

Learn more about what Dr. Cherita is up to at www.CheritaWeatherspoon.com. Connect with Cherita on Facebook® and Instagram® at CoachCherita.

ADDITIONAL RESOURCES

Love Letters to My Girls: 100+ Black Women Speak to the Hearts of Black Women & Girls

Biblical Inspiration for Black Women Entrepreneurs: A 52 Week Journey to Build Your Confidence, Align with Your purpose, and Stand in the Power of Who You Are

Avoiding the Leadership Trap: 12 Traits that Will Derail Your Career & Diminish Your Leadership Impact

Five Smooth Stones: Defeating the Giants Within

www.CheritaWeatherspoon.com